CLOTHING YOUR KIDS FOR FREE

The Ultimate Guide to Buying & Selling Your Children's Clothing

By P Jane Haynie

I0485799

Table of Contents

Forward

As a busy writer-entrepreneur and mama to two boys, one going into second grade and the other just starting to walk, I'm always a bit taken aback by the clothing and toy management aspects of raising kids (well, that and a few other things, especially with the first one!). I've been organizing, mending, and saving my older boy's clothes for over six years to be ready for the much-anticipated second baby, and let me tell you, it's been quite a project.

When Jane asked if I'd read her book about clothing your kids for free, I jumped on the opportunity to learn some new tips and tricks that I might have overlooked. As a creative, strategic type, I always love to learn new and better ways to do things and get the most bang for my buck.

See, I WANT to make the most of the awesome hand-me-downs and clothing gifts we receive, and I love the idea of being able to parlay them into future clothing as well, but so far, my own best strategies for that haven't worked out so well. It seems like I do endless amounts of sorting, storing, stain-removing, mending, schlepping to consignment stores, looking up consignment rules, etc., and I end up questioning myself about whether or not I'm getting enough of a return on my efforts to make it all worthwhile.

Plus, if I'm honest with myself, I'd love to be able to spend a little money on some nice clothes for my kids and feel like that money is actually *going somewhere* and not just being eaten by the machine. I tend to try to hold out for gratefully accepted big bags of hand-me-downs, but this book made me feel like I wouldn't just be throwing my money away if I bought wisely.

And what I discovered reading Jane's book is that there *are* some simple, small, and smart choices I can make about where to buy clothes that will work for me. She changed my mind right away about where to shop and what to buy. Who knew that buying the cheapest generic brands isn't necessarily the best move?!

I was also inspired to check out her preferred choice for selling kid's clothes – it wasn't at all what I had expected nor had I heard of it. And like I said, I always love to learn something new! Plus she threw in a bonus idea for another method as a backup if her main recommendation doesn't work for a specific location. Both of them look like terrific, fun options to explore.

One thing that hasn't changed for me is this: It's clear that it's still a commitment to manage my kid's clothing. But Jane empowered me to make my efforts fun, practical, and educated – I have a new sense of savvy and confidence that I have a real system that works to make the most of what I do with my kid's clothes.

Next I'm hoping she'll write a book about toy management! And maybe even one about women's clothes – wouldn't that be a treat. :)

In the meantime, I hope you enjoy this fast, fun read that will inspire you and get you thinking about how you buy, take care of, and ultimately pass on your kid's clothes.

- Jenna Avery www.CalledtoWrite.com San Francisco Bay Area, California

Introduction

Well hello there! Welcome to this amazing, inspiring, and bone-crunchingly innovative (or maybe at least one of those?) e-book on clothing your kids for free. Actually, it doesn't involve anything you can't already do, but it *is* pretty creative and a system I've been implementing ever since my second child was born (took me a good 4 years of testing with my first to get it right!). The landscape of buying and selling children's clothing is a bit crowded and sometimes confusing so I'm going to clear things up by teaching you the exact steps to paying absolutely $0 on clothes for your kids.

Let me start by telling you how I first discovered this system. My daughter was about 2 years old when I realized how much I was over-spending on her clothes – which is unfortunate because you lose the most money in their first year with all those growth spurts. Both my husband and I were working full-time while raising her so I began looking around to find some simple ways to "get rid" of some of her old stuff without just giving it away. I suppose I'm an enterprising person at heart, and even though I think giving freely is wonderful, I can't help but strive for efficiency and savings wherever possible.

Lucky for you!

So I started with the standard protocol: I sold clothes at garage sales and consignment stores. It seemed to work ok, but I could only get maybe fifty cents per item of clothing at a garage sale and the consignment stores only took a few of my items. I'd typically be left hauling my huge bag of clothes back home again with a measly $5 to show for my efforts. At the time I was still buying my daughter's clothes at retail sales – the lower end brands, not the designer brands – spending a bundle, and it seemed impossible that I'd ever be able to recoup that.

And that's when I came up with *"The System"* (insert evil laugh here).

You'll learn the details throughout this book, but, in a nutshell, I figured out how to obtain high quality clothes (including designer brands) for my kids at a fraction of retail price and then resell them for the same price – sometimes more! One of my first test runs included a pair of OshKosh snowpants, a Calvin Klein jacket, and a pair of Gymboree pants with the tags still on. All together, they had cost me about $11; I resold them for $20.

Ha! I was so excited!! With practice, I developed a set of rules and a process for myself that kept me on-track to continue recouping every dollar I spent on kids' clothing without ever having to track my spending or earnings.

Are you ready? Are you sure? Maybe take a drink of water first… hydrated now? Ok, let's do this.

Here's a little background to boost your confidence in my competence in this arena: I've been working in sales and marketing for almost 10 years. I studied Advertising at the University of Colorado in Boulder which had a very comprehensive, very professional advertising program taught by former employees of some of the biggest ad agencies in New York and LA (gorgeous campus too, by the way, if you ever happen upon Boulder, CO in your travels).

After college I worked for consumer goods retailers, entertainment companies, engineering firms, and my own business in the music industry. I've seen marketing from many different angles. I've brainstormed ideas for the next "sale" or promotion or campaign. I've built and executed them. And I've also been a consumer participating in them – and realized how useless they often are (let's just say there's a reason I don't do retail marketing anymore).

So I'm combining my years of sales & marketing expertise with many years as a clothing-purchasing connoisseur to teach you how to take advantage of the current buying & selling landscape, and clothe your kids for free! Please be aware that this advice applies primarily to the United States, although certainly many of the tips I provide could be implemented anywhere.

This e-book is split into 4 chapters:

Chapter 1: Setting the Landscape

This chapter gives a good solid overview of what the buying and selling landscape looks like right now so you have a framework to apply the tactics we'll talk about in later chapters. It will challenge your current thinking about how you purchase & sell clothes and rewire you to look at this issue in a more practical and profitable way.

Chapter 2: How to Buy

This chapter covers the techniques of buying clothes for your kids based on the material covered in Chapter 1. This will include an overview of how to set buying limits for yourself, a list of the various brands you should aim for, and a few other key points that will guide your purchasing.

Chapter 3: How to Sell

In order to know how to effectively spend money on kids' clothes, you've got to work out how much you can sell them for and how to do it in the most profitable way. This chapter walks you through those steps and helps you work out your selling prices. We'll discuss a particular clothing franchise I use almost exclusively to sell my kids' clothes, and circle up with the techniques learned in Chapter 2.

Chapter 4: Conclusion

A summary of everything we've discussed including a synopsis of the main points.

Chapter 1:

Setting the Landscape

First things first. There is one overall principle that informs the world of buying and selling any item and it applies equally to children's clothing:

Buy Low, Sell High.

Right? Now, obviously in our case we're not necessarily looking to make a profit here, but as you will see, clothing your kids for free requires some smart decision-making that benefits from regularly buying low and selling at or above purchase price. So we will implement this principle as thoroughly as possible.

As I mentioned earlier, the landscape of buying and selling children's clothes is crowded and confusing. To clear the air, I want to give you a brief synopsis of all the options currently available to you along with the pros and cons of each. In Chapters 2 and 3, I'll explain which ones you're going to use as part of *The System* (cue mysterious organ music).

Let's start by looking at your buying options, then the incentives that these buying options give you. The latter is important because one of the biggest challenges to clothing your kids for free is understanding which incentives are giving you a great deal, and which ones simply give you the *impression* you're getting a great deal. The world of retail sales is clever, so pay attention!

Places to buy children's clothing

Remember earlier when I mentioned my background in marketing? Well, here are a few things I've learned from being on both sides of the consumer goods industry. These vital tips will help you determine the stores to avoid when shopping for clothes:

First of all, let me tell you that we marketers aren't as bad as you think. When it comes to advertising and building promotions, the overall goal for most companies is to provide value for both the company and the consumer by coming up with innovative and creative ways of approaching business. Yes, there are certainly companies out there that are completely self-involved, but particularly in the internet age, it's incredibly difficult to last very long without genuine concern for your consumers.

But, of course, at the end of the day, a business has to conduct business. They have to make money to pay their bills, their employees, and fund any additional value they hope to provide. So just because they legitimately want to give you the best value possible, it isn't necessarily an indication that there isn't better value to be found elsewhere (wow, how many double negatives was that in one sentence? 1, 2, 3... I hope my boss never reads this...). The best business model wins. And the smartest consumer wins.

Ironically, I think any one of today's top retailers could build an empire around this pre-owned clothing purchasing trend we're entering into, but that's a discussion I'll have when the CEO of a certain big box retailer calls me back.

What I'm really saying is this: brand name and big box retailers aren't trying to cheat you, but they also don't provide the best avenues for obtaining good quality clothes for your kids at inexpensive prices. And they certainly (currently – I have high hopes for my conversations with Target) *don't* have any options that would allow you to clothe your kids for free – at least not without going out of business completely.

So with that in mind, here is the list of your options:

Retail Stores
Includes big box retailers and brand-specific stores. These are typically going to be the most expensive option.

Pros: Brand new, never-used clothing.

Cons: $$$$

Retail Outlets (Outlet Malls)
An outlet store is usually a subset location of a brand name retailer that sells the items that the retailer wasn't able to sell out of their main location. They send unsold items to the outlet and mark them down in hopes of getting something for their investment

Pros: Brand new, never-used clothing, less-expensive than at the main location

Cons: Still pretty pricey, outlets are uncommon and can often require a significant drive depending on where you live, tend to be very busy

Yard Sales
Yard sales run the other end of the spectrum from retail outlets, being one of the least expensive ways to purchase clothing.

Pros: CHEAP!!!!

Cons: Quality is hard to come by, locations are widespread and low in inventory, shopping is time-consuming

Consignment stores
These are typically locally-owned, although there are a few chains as well. They buy used items at their discretion, than increase the price to make their profit.

Pros: Less expensive than retail outlets, typically good quality, good sale prices

Cons: Locations are small and low on inventory, usually run at the higher end of the price spectrum for used clothing

Just Between Friends event-based consignment sales
Just Between Friends (JBF) is a franchise that plans and holds consignment events for both buying and selling children's items.

Pros: Inexpensive, lots of inventory in one place, 50-75% off sales, additional sale perks if you are a consignor (seller)

Cons: Because the sales are event-based, they only take place on certain dates; about once every 2-3 months per location

Thrift Stores
Ah, the ultimate bargain-shoppers' paradise. These come in either a local flavor or a chain. The chains you are likely familiar with – Goodwill, Arc, Savers, etc.

Pros: The chains have large amounts of inventory all in one place, predictable sales, name brands and designer brands are often available, as well as great prices

Cons: Inventory isn't very well regulated so items need to be inspected, sorting through the inventory can be time-consuming

Gifts/giveaways
What I'm referring to here are gifts given to you for birthdays and other occasions as well as bags of clothes given to you by other people whose kids have grown.

Pros: Duh, they're free!

Cons: There really aren't any! If you don't like them or they are in poor shape, just donate them.

Does that lay out the spread of buying options for you? Good. Now let's talk about the incentives these buying options offer to get you in to shop.

Incentives offered

Retail locations and outlet store sales

This refers to any normal sale a store holds for clothing that is currently in-season. People tend to flock to these sales, particularly on Black Friday, to get a premium price on brand new items. Here's the problem: retailers often were never selling any of their clothes at the "original price" in the first place.

Tagged prices are myths. The tagged price is there to give you the feeling that the sale price offers you big savings (they're appealing to intuition), but they never intended to sell the item for the original price anyways. So....you're actually paying original price under the guise of a sale. Tricky, right? I suppose it's not a bad thing that they want you to feel good about your purchase, but it's vitally important for you to know that that sale is likely not even real. It's there for show.

Retail and outlet off-season sales

Off-season sales used to be my bread and butter. I loved running into a particular mall-friendly children's clothing place to shop their $3 shirts, $7 pants, and $5 whatever else they had in the back of the store. It took a few years to realize I wasn't really saving much.

Yes, they probably cost less than they did at the beginning of the season, but now that I pay less than $4 for most any item of clothing I buy, I recognize that this just isn't a great deal.

Retail clearance rack

Clearance sales are usually more reliable than regular sales; they are usually legitimately trying to get rid of some stock they weren't able to sell. The problem is, the prices still aren't great. Using the spending limits we will discuss in Chapter 2, you'll learn that clearance items simply don't cut the cake when it comes to buying quality clothing on the cheap.

That said, there *may* be times when a big box retailer will have a ridiculously low-price clearance rack and it may be worth picking up a few things. But remember, this is *rare*. For example, I stocked up on tank tops and summer shorts for my daughter at a certain store the other day because they were on clearance for $1. Good sale! Even if I donate them, I'm really not losing anything. But most of the time, clearance shirts run higher than that. Since I have some guidelines I follow, I leave those ones on the rack. You'll learn to do that too.

Consignment store sales

Consignment stores don't always have the best deals unless you are buying the big stuff – cribs, bouncers, toys, changing tables, etc. In those cases, they are fantastic. They just don't tend to be great for clothes – at least not if you want to clothe your kids for free. Why? Think about it: they've got to buy used clothing at a low enough price to make a profit, however they have to pay out enough to encourage people to sell to them. Then they have to price each item even higher to make a profit.

By the time one of their items hits the rack, it's usually not a whole lot cheaper than a clearance sale. It makes it very difficult to meet your spending limits.

However, if you can catch a sale – particularly an off-season sale – you can win big!
I went to one with a 75% off winter sale in April and every item was 75 cents or less. That's even better than thrift store prices!

Just Between Friends (JBF) sale days

The beauty of shopping at a JBF sale is that on the last day or two of the sale, most locations will have a 25%-off and/or 50%-off sale on select items. If you sign up as a consignor and sell your items at the sale, you can even participate in a 75%-off sale on all donated items before they are sent to charity. Great opportunity to save big if you can keep your schedule open those days!

Thrift store sales

These can be a lot of fun. Most chain thrift stores will hold a weekly sale, usually on Saturday. At my personal favorite thrift store, Arc, they tag all their clothes with 5 different tag colors and then hold a 50% off sale for 4 of the tag colors on Saturday. Considering the items are already priced incredibly low, this is a fantastic opportunity to get a head start on clothing your kids for free.

That sums up the buyers market pretty well. This information should give you a pretty good start on where you want to spend your time as a shopper, but we'll delve into the details of my recommendations in the next chapter. Our next item to cover is selling options. We'll go through the choices available in the market today and their pros and cons as we did with buying options.

Places to sell children's clothing

Yard Sales

Yard or Garage Sales have been the I Ching of selling your kids clothes for years. Though this is not the case anymore, this technique does have its benefits.

Pros: You don't have to leave your house to sell your stuff, you receive a 100% return on sales, and it involves a relatively small amount of prep

Cons: Margins are tiny (sale prices are usually 50 cents or less per item), you have to execute your own marketing, and you are at the mercy of whoever happens to show up to shop.

Consignment Stores

These small shops are known as being a prime spot for selling children's clothes (and, as I mentioned before, they are great for the big stuff like cribs, swings, and changing tables), but there are some definite downsides to spending time using this resource.

Pros: They are typically fair in their payout, you can shop while they're going through your stuff

Cons: They don't take very many items from each seller so you will likely end up hauling most of it back out to your car, it can take hours sometimes for them to comb through all of your stuff, and because of the small amount of items they take, your payout is almost always small

Just Between Friends event-based consignment sales

In addition to buying clothes at JBF, you can also sell your gently-used children's clothing there.

Pros: JBF sets up a huge event to hold thousands of pieces of clothing, they handle all of the marketing and provide the shoppers, you get to choose your selling prices, you keep the lion's share of your sales, and most of your preparation can be executed while your kids are with you

Cons: Some preparation is involved, and you are subject to the event schedule

Online Portals/Auction Sites

There are various places you can sell your items online, I'm sure you're aware of the major ones. Some of them are auction sites, some have simple listings, and there are even some to which you can ship your items in return for a check at their discretion.

Pros: They are simple to use, and can reach a large number of potential buyers.

Cons: You will likely have to lump your clothing into "lots" and then sell at a low price to get any interest so margins are therefore low, sometimes you have to work out how to cover shipping, and they aren't common portals for selling clothes so it's difficult to find interest.

Your own locally organized event

I'll go into more detail on this in Chapter 3, but if the other recommended selling options are unavailable, this is certainly on the table if you're willing to put in the effort required to organize, advertise, and fund this type of thing.

Pros: You do it your way, you keep all your profits, you give lots of other people opportunities to sell their kids' clothing

Cons: It's a *lot* of work and it's up to you to execute everything accurately and on-schedule

Got it? Good! You've now graduated from the informational section of this e-book. Understanding the landscape in which you're working will go miles to help you make informed choices about where you buy and where you sell.

Chapter 2:

How to Buy

Ugh, I know, this is such a stupid chapter title. Everybody knows how to buy clothes, how to save money, and how to hit the sales, right? Well, not really. There's a chance you might already know these secrets and this book could be redundant for you, but more than likely you *think* you know the secrets but you've actually bought into the secrets retailers *want* you to believe. Ever heard the saying "what is popular is not always right, and what is right is not always popular"? Implement that concept here.

I want to start this chapter by going over some general guidelines I've pulled from the information presented to you in Chapter 1. This synopsis will give you the starting block from which to make your choices.

Forget about buying new

It's fine on special occasions, but for the majority of the clothes you purchase for your kids, let go of trips to the shopping mall. Strike it from the record, it ain't happenin' no more. Buying clothes new is the number one way to completely throw away your money.

My kids walk around almost exclusively in name brand clothing, some of which was bought with the tags still on, but I don't think I've ever bought them from a name-brand retail outlet of any kind. You don't need new. New is Foo! Repeat this to yourself.

Scratch the words "Sale" and "Clearance" from your psyche

This applies in a retail context primarily, but as of now, these words are no longer in your vocabulary. Hold a funeral for them if you have to, but get rid of them. In fact, based on these first two points, you should pretty much never plan on stepping foot into the kids' clothing section of a big box or brand name retailer ever again.

Geez, Jane, harsh much?

Perhaps. But it will pay off.

Set buying limits for yourself

We'll talk more about this later, but you need to set spending limits for certain types of clothes and brands depending on how much you can sell them for. Clothing your kids for free isn't necessarily about buying cheap as much as it is about buying for an equal or lower price than you can sell. Cheaper is only better if the item is of high enough quality to re-sell later.

Got it? Good. I also have a few nuggets of information I'd like to share that are going to be very helpful for you based on general trends I've observed that I think are notable. They are:

- Girls' clothing sells better than boys' clothing
- Dresses & skirts sell better than pants and shirts
- Clothing sell-ability <u>decreases</u> with age (you will find it hard to sell anything after your kids turn 6 or 7)
- Babies clothing sizes 0-6m offers the highest profit margins
- Formal clothing sells a little bit better than casual clothing, but not by much
- Winter coats and snowpants are a <u>cash cow</u>

Okay! We've got a good foundation now and you have an idea what you're getting into. Let's dive into *The System*! (dum, dum, duuuuuuuuuuuum) (That's dramatic music in case you couldn't tell).

Let's talk about (1) spending limits since this is one of the key principles of my system. After that, we'll go through the limits on (2) where to buy, (3) when to buy, and (4) what to buy.

Spending limits

Why set spending limits? If you want to avoid keeping spreadsheets of everything you buy and sell, you'll need to put a cap on how much you're willing to shell out for any particular item of clothing. This way when it comes time to sell, you can always say to yourself "Well, I know I didn't spend more than $x on it" and then price it accordingly.

I accomplish this by setting specific maximum dollar amounts that I'm willing to spend on each type of clothing. Before

I get into the details, please keep in mind that every market is different. The market I've tested is Denver, CO but I guarantee the details will be different in San Francisco, CA and Raleigh, NC. These numbers will give you a starting point, however, from which you can begin testing to build your own Buying Limits spreadsheet.

Here we go! Following is the table I use to guide my purchasing. The values I recommend here are based off of the maximum each clothing item can be sold for using the methods I will describe in Chapter 3. The table is separated into "Name Brands" and "Designer Brands". If you are unsure what these categories mean, examples will be provided in Chapter 3. As you can see, "Generic Brands" are not an included category. This is because you won't be purchasing generic brands anymore. I'll explain more on that later. Again, use this as a starting point rather than an exhaustive list:

Clothing type	Name Brand	Designer Brand
T-shirts – short and long-sleeve	$1	$1
Knit shirts	$3	$7
Slacks	$3	$6
Shorts	$2	$4
Denim jeans	$3	$5
Casual pants (cargo pants, for example)	$2	$3
Cardigans	$3	$6
Button-up shirts	$3	$5
Jackets	$6	$10
Coats	$10	$15
Dresses	$6	$8
Skirts	$3	$5
Formal Dresses	$7	$9
Formal Shirts	$3	$5
Formal Skirts	$4	$6
Sandals	$1	$1
Casual Shoes	$3	$7
Dress Shoes	$3	$5
Sneakers	$3	$3
Boots	$4	$6

As you can see, in most instances your buying limit for designer brands will be higher than your buying limit for name brands. However, there are cases where your buying limit for name brands and designer brands are the same. My experience has taught me that the items that tend to sell the least effectively (t-shirts, sneakers, and sandals) consistently sell poorly in any brand category. My general advice would be to avoid buying in these areas altogether, but let's face it – kids need sneakers and sandals! So stay as low as possible on the buying side for these items (under $1, if possible), and be prepared to price them low as well regardless of brand name.

To reiterate the basic concept here, adjust these numbers as-needed for your particular market so you always know the most you're willing to spend on any particular item. It will keep glitter, sequins, and patent leather from swaying your objectivity.

Where to buy

I'm going to make this very easy for you. Below is the list I gave you in Chapter 1. As you can see, the selling locations I recommend using my system are bold, while the places you shouldn't touch with a ten-foot pole are crossed out. If you need further explanation on the reasons for these decisions, please refer to Chapter 1.

- ~~Retail Stores~~
- ~~Retail Outlets (Outlet Malls)~~
- ~~Yard Sales~~
- ~~Consignment stores~~
- **Just Between Friends event-based consignment sales**
- **Thrift Stores**
- **Gifts/giveaways**

Simple, right? I do want to throw in two quick important tips here for thrift stores since you have a variety of locations to buy from – and they are *not* all created equal.

Tips & Tricks: Thrift Stores

Shop the chains

Avoid the locally-owned thrift stores. I'm a huge fan of shopping locally normally, but it doesn't fit our purposes here. If you want to pay nothing for the clothes you buy for children, stick to the chain thrift stores. They have more bandwidth to offer low prices, and they have more predictable pricing and sales incentives. My personal favorite is Arc due to their large selection, name brands, and great sales, but do some exploring to identify your favorite.

Shop in high-end neighborhoods

I really hate this reality, but the poorer the neighborhood, the lower the quality of clothing in the local thrift store. Most big cities have several different chain thrift stores scattered throughout the metro area; find the one with best stuff on a regular basis.

How do you know? For some cities this is pretty obvious. For others it may not be. For example, in the Denver area Highlands Ranch is known as one of the yuppiest towns to live in, but I've always found the best clothing at the thrift stores in Loveland. Look around. Here are a few indicators that you've got a gem:

- You can find at *least* 3 or 4 items with the original tags still on

- "Designer Brands" can be found if you dig (here's that list I promised you), such as:
  - Calvin Klein
  - Janie and Jack
  - Any high end outdoor brands (Columbia, Prana, etc)
  - Kenneth Cole
  - Billieblush
  - Ralph Lauren
  - Urban Sunday
  - Google "designer children's clothing" to get a more comprehensive list

- "Name Brands" can be found easily, for example

- Gymboree
- OshKosh
- GAP
- Old Navy
- Adidas
- Children's Place
- Winnie the Pooh
- Disney

- Generic brands are in shorter supply (although most thrift stores will have at least 50% generic brands, usually more so be prepared for that).

As for the types of sales and clearance promotions we discussed in Chapter 1, only shop those associated with these three buying locations, with the exception of Consignment Store sales. As we discussed already, those can be excellent, just exercise caution. So retail outlet sales, off-season sales, and clearance racks are now out.

"Strike that from the record!"

Thwack!

On to the next!

When to buy

We've determined so far that the only places you're shopping are JBF sales, thrift stores, and by receiving gifts. We won't cover receiving gifts because that's a given, but let's talk about the best times to shop at JBF sales and thrifts stores.

JBF sales

This is going to be pretty simple, but here it goes: first, shop during the week of the sale before the sale prices kick in. The reason I suggest this is because there are a lot of people who price their items much, much lower than you'd expect; you want to be the first person to the rack to snag them. Not all items are going to be marked for clearance on the sale days so take advantage of the opportunity grab the best stuff early on. Second, shop during the 25%, 50%, and/or 75%-off sales. Since JBF is on your list of places to sell your items as well, take advantage of the consignors-only 75%-off sale if your franchise offers it.

Thrift stores

Some of you will love this suggestion and some of you will hate it: you're going to need to shop pretty regularly at the thrift store. And by "regularly", I mean every Saturday. If this bothers you, consider sticking to JBF sales for your purchases. Because unless your town's thrift store has a different schedule, Saturday is hands-down the best day to get the best deals at most thrift stores.

But Jane, why do I need to shop every Saturday? My kids don't need clothes every Saturday.

Well, that's true, but thrift store inventory is unpredictable and you need to be open to buying your son's future winter coat in April and his summer swimsuit in January. There's no way of knowing which Saturday shopping trip will yield the deals you need to meet your goals. The good news, though, is that you can usually find at least a few things for the current season that fit your criteria on each trip. So as you get better, you won't have to go as often.

What to buy

Here's the biggie, and this one is *soooooooooo* important so pay attention to this section. You are going to suddenly become very picky about what you choose to buy for your kids.

Stick to name brands and designer brands

The first BIG secret to clothing your kids for free is this: don't buy generic. I know, it goes against all wisdom, doesn't it? You've spent your life convincing yourself that generic brands are just as good as name brands, the tag on the shirt doesn't matter, it's better to save the money, etc. On a philosophical level, of course, this is true. But despite being aware of this, the kind of shoppers you're going to be selling to are going to be just like you – thrilled to get a deal on something. And they're going to be even *more* thrilled when they can get a nice used name brand outfit at a price lower than the new generics!

So trust me on this one. It's not so much about how much you pay as it is about how much you can sell it for. Thrifty shoppers don't mess with generics.

Pay Attention to Style and Color

Always, always, always, buy clothing in eye-catching colors and designs. The more adorable, the better. The brighter, the better. Humans are visual creatures and when your clothes are sitting on a rack with 100's of others, you've got to catch a person's eye. Trust me, if you aren't waving something shiny and bright, *they won't see it*. Following this guideline will get your items out of your hands faster and at a larger return.

Make sure items are clean

By clean, I mean without spots or stains. Take a good look. Hold the items up to the light. Pay attention to the most accident-prone spot: the collar. Even on white colors it can sometimes be hard to see a yellow stain at first glance. If you think you can get a stain out, that's your prerogative, but I would avoid the hassle when possible.

Chapter 3:

How to Sell

Now we get into the meat of the book! Let's look at our "Places to sell" list from Chapter 1:

- ~~Yard Sales~~
- ~~Consignment Stores~~
- **Just Between Friends event-based consignment sales**
- ~~Online Portals/Auction Sites~~
- **Your own locally organized event**

Ha, well that makes things easy, doesn't it? There's really only one place I've found to be both profitable and efficient for selling children's clothing: JBF is it. As you can see, organizing your own local event is also an option, but I would only suggest that under two circumstances:

1) **There is no JBF event within a 2-hour drive**
   For the amount of time and money you save by letting JBF do all the marketing, set-up, and organization for you, it's worth the drive if there's an event within an hour of your town. You could stock up on clothes and go only twice a year if you want.

2) **You really enjoy organizing and running your own events, you are well-networked, and you are marketing-savvy.**
   If this kind of thing is fun for you, and you think you can pull it off, go for it! Just be aware of all the balls you have to keep in the air and the number of people you will need to reach to make it worthwhile.

Otherwise, stick to JBF. I know, I know, it's hard to believe that those are the *only* options out there that are worthwhile, but take a look at our other choices again:

Yard Sales: at 25-50 cents per item, the earnings simply aren't there.

Consignment Stores: As we discussed earlier, you may get a decent return for your clothes, but you'll only be able to sell 10-20% of them; you'll have to make trips to 7 or 8 different stores to get anywhere near 50%.

Online Portals/Auction Sites: Other than the obvious auction and listing sites – which, as I mentioned before, are ineffective and low margin – I've looked at a few other options and, trust me, they are not worth it. I sent a huge bag of stuff into one online store thinking I'd get at least $20 out of it and I only got $3.50!

Seriously, the only other option out there *that works* and offers you maximum profit for minimum effort is the Just Between Friends franchise (please note: I do not have any financial ties to the JBF franchise other than the $100's of dollars I've made selling my kids' clothing there. I do not own or have any relation to anyone who owns one of the franchises. I'm writing about it here simply because it's awesome!) It exists nationwide so chances are there is an event happening near you.

So let's start there with some major time- and money-saving tips and then we'll talk briefly about your back-up options if there is no JBF in your area.

Selling at JBF

1) Go online to www.jbfsale.com and sign up for an account. From there you can register for an event in your area as a shopper, consigner, and/or volunteer. This franchise exists all over the country so even if you've never heard of it, look it up and you'll likely find one within driving distance.

2) Register as a "consignor". This means you want to sell your gently-used children's clothing at one of their events.

3) Once you've done this, you will be able to search for a local event and click "Register" to sell at that particular location.

And then the fun part begins! The site gives you a pretty good walk-through of how everything works, so be sure to follow the steps and recommendations as they are laid out for you.

I've been selling at JBF for three or four years now and I've gained some pretty useful tips and tricks that can move the process along faster, make your items stand out, and of course, make you more money. These tips are worth their weight in gold, so take notes!

Tips & Tricks: Tagging

- Print your tags on light cardstock – 60 lb or less. It's not flimsy enough to get ripped off the clothing, but still bendable enough to be pinned to the clothing.

- Complete your computer entry, printing, and tagging process in groups of 12-18 items. This way you don't end up with a huge pile of 100's of tags that you then have to match up with your huge pile of 100's of clothes.

- Buy kid-sized hangers at Wal-mart. They have them in packages of 10 for $1. Paying a mere ten cents per hanger will greatly reduce your overhead. For pants and skirts, they also have adult-sized wire hangers for the same price onto which you can safety-pin the tops of the clothing (pants hangers are way too expensive to be justified).

- Decide if you want to sell your items for half off on the last day of the sale. When you're tagging, you'll have the option to place a checkmark on items you wish to include in this promotion. I would recommend *not* using this feature the first few times you sell. You'll want to get an idea how high you can sell your items at full price first and it may take a few sales to figure that out.

Tips & Tricks: Dropping off

- When you drop off, you'll need a rolling rack to carry all your clothes and other items. The JBF sales have a limited number of these so I'd recommend buying your own. Wal-mart has a small one for $14 that typically would hold 50+ clothing items for me. It will save you time waiting for a rolling rack and make it easier (on your back!) to bring things inside.

- Before dropping your clothes off at the sale, spray them with an odor eliminator (I like Febreeze). They will smell nice and fresh!

- Combine outfits. A customer will be more likely to pay $6 for two outfits than $3 or even $2 for just one. It just *feels* like a better deal (remember that intuition we talked about earlier? Use it to your advantage).

Tips & Tricks: Pricing

- You get to keep 60-65% of your sales depending on the franchise owner. If you want 70-75% you can volunteer to help out for 4+ hours at the sale. It's typically very easy to volunteer and can even be a lot of fun!

- If you sell more than half of your items at your first sale, increase the prices 50 cents-$1 for the next one (don't do any re-tagging, just make a note to charge a little more for the next group of clothing you sell). If you sell less than half, decrease the price by the same amount.

- You will always have clothes leftover from each sale. You'll rarely sell everything, so if an item goes through 2 or 3 sales before someone buys it, it's not a big deal. If you prefer to sell more than half of your clothes at every sale, lower your pricing accordingly and make sure you adjust your purchase price as well! You'll need to buy lower to sell lower.

- You will find items on the thrift store rack that you can sell for well more than your calculated 65% return. If you can price them higher and make a profit, go for it! (Because your kids will inevitably stain some clothes, making them un-sellable, try to price above breaking-even as often as possible. Price low enough to sell, but high enough to make up for clothes that had to hit the trash).

Tips & Tricks: Calculating sell prices

Now, because of the 65% return on clothing for these kinds of sales, you'll need to figure out how much you want to sell the items for based on the total return you'd like to receive. This can be a little tricky when you're buying clothing at thrift store or JBF half-off sales, so I'll share the process I use to calculate:

1) I buy an item that cost $2, but is 50% off. So my purchase price is $1.

2) When I sell it, I need to be able to get at least $1 for it

3) Therefore, I need to set the price such that when I get my 65% commission, my pay-out on that item is at least $1.

4) To calculate this, you'll need to divide the price of the item by the 65% return you'd like: 1 / 0.65 = 1.53

5) In this case, I'd need to resell it for at least $1.53

6) If the math here doesn't make sense, work it backwards to confirm: if you sell an item at $1.53 and receive a 65% return, what is your profit? $1.53 x 0.65 = $0.9945 (or $1). Trust the formula.

7) If I think that's doable, I'll go for it. If I think I can sell it for more than $1.53 – bonus!

Hot Tip: I've even been known on occasion to buy clothes that are the wrong size for my kids and go straight to re-selling them. For example, last year I found a Van Heusen suit jacket size 4T with the tags on which listed the retail price at $60. I bought it for $6, resold it at $20. This means you can be a little more flexible with the other clothes you buy, and also prepare yourself for the inevitable stained clothes that won't be re-sellable at all.

Tips & Tricks: Cleaning kids' clothes

Now hang on a second, Jane, if I'm selling this stuff after my kids have worn it, I'm going to have to keep it clean! That sounds like an impossible endeavor!

Ok, well that's a good point. It's not always easy but it's definitely doable. It's actually a good reason to sell your clothes above the price you bought them for – that way the extra profits you get from the clean ones makes up for the dirty ones you couldn't sell. However, there are some rules I have followed that have greatly decreased my chances of having stained clothes when it came time to sell:

- Don't buy stained clothes. Duh. I know. But don't.

- Don't remove tags until your child is ready to wear the item. You never know, they might never wear it. Clothes with tags-on get snatched up much faster.

- Use bibs. Good ones that cover the neck.

- Find a really good stain remover. My favorite is Resolve Max.

- NEVER ever put clothing in the dryer with a stain; it will set. Spray it with stain remover again and put it back in the washer.

Organizing your own local event

As I mentioned before, organizing your own local event is an option you can consider if you have the skillset and desire to pull it off. Please keep in mind that I have never held one of these personally (I prefer the convenience of letting JBF do all the work!), but I do have some ideas you can use as a starting off point.

There are three forms I can see this taking, and I would suggest running any one of these at either the neighborhood or city level, depending on how large your city is.

1) **Clothing swap**
   This is your simplest option since it does not require the exchange of money. I would recommend contacting a church, park, or non-profit organization to see if they would donate space for your event; then simply advertise through as many outlets as you can access. A clothing swap simply involves a group of people bringing their kids' old clothes and bartering to make exchanges. Nobody brings money, everything is exchanged one-for-one.

2) MeetUp group

You've perhaps heard of the social media site, MeetUp. It provides a platform for organizing get-togethers for people with common interests. It seems to me this could be a great platform for building a group of local women who either would like to organize a clothing swap, or attend a kids' clothing sales event that you organize. The latter would be somewhat more complicated and will involve finding a location, identifying and hauling in tables, a cash register, and clothing racks, and setting rules and standards surrounding how the sale works. But again, you and everyone involved would keep all of your profits.

If one of these options appeals to you, give it a try! And then, hey, maybe write a book about it.

Chapter 4:

Conclusion

Go and Do!

You are now officially certified to clothe your children for free! Start by tucking the spending limits table into your purse and jotting down those brand names so you can start working out your limits while you shop.

Buying clothes for kids doesn't have to be expensive. Buying high-end clothes for kids doesn't have to be expensive. Before I started using this system, I don't think it ever occurred to me that it could even be free! I'll admit, I go through periods of time where I simply don't have the energy for this and I simply donate my kids' clothes. That's okay, because I've gotten so good at this that I *still* break even the fact that I got nothing for 10-20 items!

I hope you find this system as useful as I have. The world is changing quickly and the old tricks our parents used to buy our play clothes don't work anymore – lucky for us because clothing your kids for free was not possible even 20 years ago. My hope is that after implementing this system you will proudly grab a pen (or stylus), walk over to your budgeting spreadsheet, and vehemently scratch "Kid's Clothing" from the list.

Synopsis

Here's a quick synopsis of the main principles covered in this book:

- **Primary principle:** Buy Low, Sell High

- **Guiding recommendations**
  - Forget about buying new
  - Scratch the words "Sale" and "Clearance" from your psyche
  - Set buying limits for yourself

- **Where to buy**
  - Just Between Friends event-based consignment sales
  - Thrift Stores
  - Gifts/giveaways

- **Thrift store buying tips**
    - Shop the chains
    - Shop in high-end neighborhoods

- **Designer brand examples**
    - Calvin Klein
    - Janie and Jack
    - Any high end outdoor brands (Columbia, Prana, etc)
    - Kenneth Cole
    - Billieblush
    - Ralph Lauren
    - Urban Sunday
    - Google "designer children's clothing" to get a more comprehensive list

- **Name brand examples**
    - Gymboree
    - OshKosh
    - GAP
    - Old Navy
    - Adidas
    - Children's Place
    - Winnie the Pooh
    - Disney

- **When to buy**
    - JBF Sales: Shop during the first day(s) of the sale and during the 50%-off and 75% off sales
    - Thrift stores: Shop on Saturday as often as possible

- **What to buy**
    - Stick to name brands and designer brands
    - Pay Attention to Style and Color
    - Make sure items are clean

- **How to sell**
    - Sell only at JBF consignment event sales
    - If you don't have a JBF near you:
        - Buy the franchise and start one near you
        - Stock pile your clothes and make 1-2 trips per year
        - Set up your own local consignment sale

About the Author

P Jane Haynie is an author, marketing professional, and bargain-shopping maven. She has been writing poetry, short stories, and music compositions for 20 years, and has started several businesses – a few of which were actually successful! "Clothing Your Kids For Free" is her first breakout published work leveraging years of knowledge gained through success and failure in marketing, business, and consumer shopping. Jane lives with her husband, two children, and two dogs in Denver, CO.